Life Cycles

Life Cycle of a Chicken

by Meg Gaertner

www.focusreaders.com

Copyright © 2022 by Focus Readers®, Lake Elmo, MN 55042. All rights reserved. No part of this book may be reproduced or utilized in any form or by any means without written permission from the publisher.

Focus Readers is distributed by North Star Editions:
sales@northstareditions.com | 888-417-0195

Produced for Focus Readers by Red Line Editorial.

Photographs ©: iStockphoto, cover, 1, 7, 8, 11, 13, 14, 17, 18; Shutterstock Images, 4, 21

Library of Congress Cataloging-in-Publication Data
Names: Gaertner, Meg, author.
Title: Life cycle of a chicken / by Meg Gaertner.
Description: Lake Elmo, MN : Focus Readers, [2022] | Series: Life
  cycles | Includes index. | Audience: Grades 2-3
Identifiers: LCCN 2021003741 (print) | LCCN 2021003742 (ebook) | ISBN
  9781644938270 (hardcover) | ISBN 9781644938737 (paperback) | ISBN
  9781644939192 (ebook) | ISBN 9781644939635 (pdf)
Subjects: LCSH: Chickens--Life cycles--Juvenile literature.
Classification: LCC SF487.5 .G34 2022 (print) | LCC SF487.5 (ebook) |
  DDC 636.5--dc23
LC record available at https://lccn.loc.gov/2021003741
LC ebook record available at https://lccn.loc.gov/2021003742

Printed in the United States of America
Mankato, MN
082021

About the Author

Meg Gaertner enjoys reading, writing, dancing, and being outside. She lives in Minnesota.

Table of Contents

CHAPTER 1

Egg 5

CHAPTER 2

Embryo 9

THAT'S AMAZING!

Pipping 12

CHAPTER 3

Chick 15

CHAPTER 4

Chicken 19

Focus on Chicken Life Cycles • 22

Glossary • 23

To Learn More • 24

Index • 24

Chapter 1

Egg

A **hen** usually lays one egg each day. Sometimes, she **mates** with a **rooster**. Then the egg is **fertilized**. Only fertilized eggs grow into chickens.

The hen lays many eggs. Then she broods. This means she sits on the eggs. She broods for three weeks. She keeps each egg warm. That way, the **embryo** inside can grow.

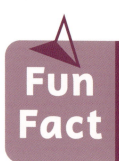 **Fun Fact** Hens lay eggs even without mating. A hen that gets more sunlight will lay more eggs.

Chapter 2

Embryo

Big changes happen inside the egg. This stage is called the embryo. The embryo uses **nutrients** inside the egg to grow.

Different body parts grow. The heart and eyes grow. The legs and wings grow, too. The embryo grows for three weeks inside the egg.

Fun Fact: The eggs people buy at the store are not fertilized. There are no embryos inside them.

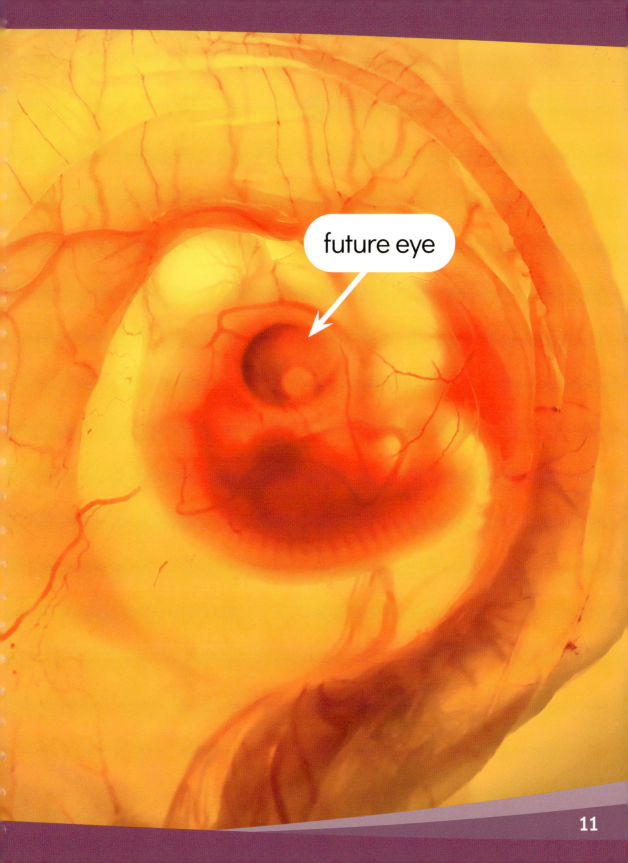

That's Amazing!

Pipping

The chick is ready to **hatch** after 19 or 20 days. Then it starts pipping. The chick pecks a hole in the egg's shell. It uses a special tooth. With each peck, the hole gets bigger. The new **hatchling** comes out of the egg. Pipping can take up to one day.

Chapter 3

Chick

Chicks come out wet. But they dry quickly. Chicks have a soft, fluffy covering. It is called down. It helps keep them warm.

Most chicks can stand and walk right away. They eat feed and drink water. The chicks get bigger. They start growing feathers.

Fun Fact Feed includes wheat, corn, and more. It has all the nutrients chicks need to grow.

Chapter 4

Chicken

Chicks grow over many weeks.
Their bodies are skinny at first.
But they soon fill out. Chicks
also grow their adult feathers.

Male and female chickens look different. Roosters have large, colorful **combs** on their heads. Hens often have shorter tail feathers. The hens start laying eggs. Hens and roosters mate. Some eggs are fertilized. The life cycle goes on.

Life Cycle Stages

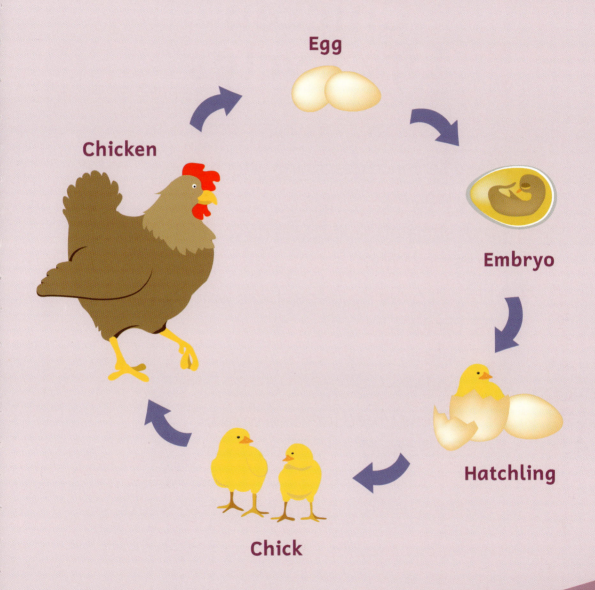

21

FOCUS ON
Chicken Life Cycles

Write your answers on a separate piece of paper.

1. Write a sentence describing what happens during pipping.

2. Which stage of the life cycle do you find most interesting? Why?

3. What soft covering keeps chicks warm?
   - A. combs
   - B. down
   - C. feathers

4. Why do hens brood for three weeks?
   - A. Chicks hatch after three weeks.
   - B. Chicks grow feathers after three weeks.
   - C. Hens and roosters mate for three weeks.

Answer key on page 24.

Glossary

combs
Growths on the heads of chickens, usually larger on roosters.

embryo
A stage of growth that happens before birth or hatching.

fertilized
Able to grow a new animal.

hatch
To come out of an egg.

hatchling
A young animal that just came out of its egg.

hen
A female chicken, able to lay eggs.

mates
Comes together to make a baby.

nutrients
Things that people, animals, and plants need to stay healthy.

rooster
A male chicken, unable to lay eggs.

To Learn More

BOOKS

London, Martha. *Baby Chickens*. Minneapolis: Abdo Publishing, 2021.

Tonkin, Rachel, and Stephanie Fizer Coleman. *Egg to Chicken*. New York: Crabtree Publishing, 2019.

NOTE TO EDUCATORS

Visit **www.focusreaders.com** to find lesson plans, activities, links, and other resources related to this title.

Index

C
chick, 12, 15–16, 19, 21

E
embryo, 6, 9–10, 21

H
hen, 5–6, 20

N
nutrients, 9, 16

P
pipping, 12

R
rooster, 5, 20

Answer Key: 1. Answers will vary; **2.** Answers will vary; **3.** B; **4.** A